The Coolest Pets

Dogs

Anne O'Daly

KidHaven PUBLISHING

Published in 2024 by
KidHaven Publishing, an Imprint of Greenhaven Publishing, LLC
2544 Clinton St., Buffalo, NY 14224

Portions of this work were originally authored by Dawn Titmus and published as *Dogs*.
All new material this edition authored by Anne O'Daly.

Design Manager: Keith Davis
Picture Manager: Sophie Mortimer

Photo Credits:
Front Cover: Shutterstock: Nynke van Holten b, Odua Images tr; Thinkstock: iStock tl, bl.
Interior: iStock: andresr 8/9, andyworks 18t, baramee2554 7tr, Bigandt Photograhy 27t, busypix 6br, cynoclub 3, 15br, 22–23, 24–25, 26–27, Fat Camera 5cl, Fenne 25b, fotoedu 11tr, GlobalP 4–5, 25br, Kali9 19b, 25t, Ryan J Lane 7br, LeslieLauren 29t, lleerogers 6bc, Maica 13b, mauinow1 13t, mehmettoriak 7c, Deniz Murat 12–13, nimu1956 18b, papound 7cr, SeventyFour 17, tderen 14l, THEPALMER 21t, valeryg 4cl, yellowsarah 19c; Shutterstock: Anneka 15t, Bolt Photo 29cr, Casteco Design 28, cynoclub 10–11, FabrikaSint 14b, Jack Jelly 9c, Budmin Jeutic 23t, kurashova 29bl, Dorottya Mathe 1, 16–17, schubbel 16, Rin Seiko 23b, Sladic 11tr, Sundays Photography 27b, Helen Sushitskaya 21b; Thinkstock: amactor 9t, GlobalP 20, Lucato 9b, malamooshi 12bl, Padrin7 8.
T=top, b=bottom, l=left, r=right, c=center

Cataloging-in-Publication Data

Names: O'Daly, Anne
Title: Dogs / Anne O'Daly.
Description: Buffalo, New York : Kidhaven Publishing, 2024. |
Series: The coolest pets| Includes index and glossary
Identifiers: ISBN 9781534545359 (pbk) | ISBN 9781534545366 (library bound) | ISBN 9781534545373 (ebook)
Subjects: LCSH: Dogs-- Juvenile literature | Pets--Juvenile literature
Classification: LCC SF426.5 O33 2024 | DDC 636.7--dc23

Manufactured in the United States of America

CPSIA compliance information: Batch #CSKH24: For further information contact Greenhaven Publishing LLC at 1-844-317-7404.

Please visit our website, www.greenhavenpublishing.com.
For a free color catalog of all our high-quality books, call toll free 1-844-317-7404 or fax 1-844-317-7405.

Find us on

Contents

Choosing a Dog

Dogs make great pets. They are loyal and fun. There are many breeds to choose from, and lots of gorgeous dogs who are a mix of different breeds. All dogs need love, care, and attention.

Home and Lifestyle

A dog needs to fit into your family's lifestyle. Dogs are social animals. They love company. Will the dog be left alone much, or will someone be home to keep it company? Do you have a backyard or do you live in an apartment? Some dogs get along well with other pets. Others like to be the only pet. Dogs such as terriers are bred to chase small animals. They are more likely to run after cats and small furry animals.

Young or Old?

Puppies need a lot of attention and training. You will have to housebreak a puppy and spend lots of time with it at first. An older dog may be better suited to your family.

Checklist

- Will the dog have company during the day?
- Do you have the time to give an active dog lots of exercise every day?
- Can your family afford the food costs and vet bills?
- Do you have another pet in the home?

Adopt a Dog

Rescue centers are full of dogs and puppies that need new homes. Check your local center to see if you can give a pet a forever home before you look for a breeder.

Next Steps

Dogs are great pets and make loyal companions, but it is important to choose the right one for you. This book will help you to pick and care for your pet. Learn about four of the most family-friendly breeds. Try your hand at making some tasty doggy cookies. You will also find some fascinating facts about your new best friend!

Getting Started

Before you bring your new companion home, you'll need a few basic items. These include food and water bowls, a collar and leash, and some toys. Your dog will also need a bed or crate to sleep in.

Checklist

- Food and water bowls the right size for your dog.
- Collar with ID tag and a leash.
- Grooming brushes and comb.
- Pooper-scooper and poop bags. The law says you must pick up after your pooch!
- Toys, such as tug-of-war rope, chew toys, balls, and ball thrower.
- Bed and crate for sleeping.

Dog Bowls

Food and water bowls should be large enough for your dog to get its mouth inside easily. Nonslip bases on bowls are useful, so your pooch does not push its food around the floor!

Brush and Comb

All dogs need grooming–some more than others. You will need a brush and comb especially for your dog. A slicker brush has small pins on it. They are good for getting tangles out of hair. An ordinary bristle brush is good for giving the coat shine.

ID Tag and License

In most states, dogs must have a license. Your dog's collar should have an ID tag with the license number attached. If your dog goes missing, a license tag helps animal control get your dog back to you.

Microchips

A microchip is placed under your dog's skin. The chip has a number that identifies your dog. If your dog goes missing and is found by someone, animal control scans the chip to read the number.

Collar vs. Harness

If a dog pulls on the leash, the collar can put pressure on its neck and cause injury. A harness can be a better way to keep control of your dog on walks. A harness can help stop a dog pulling on the leash. Make sure you fit the right size harness for your dog.

Food and Drink

Your dog needs a healthy, balanced diet to keep it happy and well. The amount of food depends on its diet, size, and age. Your pet also needs a constant supply of clean drinking water.

How Much Food

Read the label on your dog's food to find out how much to give. The amount depends on your dog's weight. Make sure you measure your dog's food. Ask an adult to check your dog's weight every two to three weeks. If your dog is gaining or losing weight, you'll need to adjust the amount of food or exercise it has.

Chews are tasty treats.

Treats

Treats are a great way to reward good behavior when you are training your dog. You can buy special dog treats in a pet store. Most dogs also like small pieces of cheese and cooked chicken. Be careful not to give your dog too many treats!

Foods to Avoid

Some human foods are poisonous for dogs. Never feed your dog grapes, onion, avocado, rhubarb, fruits with pits such as peaches, or mushrooms. Chocolate can be poisonous, too. Baker's chocolate is more toxic than milk or white chocolate.

Which Kind of Food?

Some people like to feed their dogs canned food. Other people prefer to give kibble (dried food). You can also feed your dog a mixture of both. Make sure to give the right amounts for your dog's weight, age, and daily activity. Puppies need to be fed three or more times a day. Adult dogs should eat one or two meals a day.

Kibble (dried food)

Canned meat meal

Complete dried food

Cleaning and Grooming

Whatever type of dog you have, you need to brush it regularly. Almost all dogs shed hair. Many breeds molt twice every year. Some breeds do not molt, but their coats need to be groomed and clipped regularly.

Clean Teeth

Just like people, dogs need to have clean, healthy teeth. Ask an adult to help you clean your dog's teeth. You will need special toothpaste made for dogs–don't use ordinary toothpaste. You can use an old toothbrush or a finger brush. You may need to get your dog used to you handling its mouth at first. Pull up the dog's lips and brush the teeth gently. Work from front to back.

Bathtime

If you need to give your dog a bath, use a mild baby shampoo or a special shampoo for dogs. Make sure you rinse all the shampoo out with warm water. Have a dog towel ready for the big shake-off!

Getting Rid of Tangles

Use a comb or slicker brush to detangle your dog's coat. Comb out any dead hair from the undercoat. Then brush the coat, starting at your dog's head and working toward the back. Gently brush your dog's chest and tummy area. Brush down the legs to the feet.

Ticks and Fleas

Ask an adult to help check and remove any ticks. Ticks carry diseases. If you see flea dirt–small, dark specks on the skin–ask an adult to give your dog some anti-flea treatment.

Exercise

Dogs need exercise to stay healthy and in shape. Some breeds, such as collies and retrievers, need a couple of hours of exercise a day. Others, such as a Great Dane, are happy on the couch. Most dogs need two or three walks a day.

Fun and Games

Lots of dogs love to play. Retrievers enjoy playing fetch games with a ball or favorite toy. Terriers were bred to find rats or foxes, so they often like to dig. Mental stimulation is also important. Brain games will stop your dog from getting bored. Try hiding its food or a favorite toy.

Off Leash

Dogs love being free to explore off the leash. They will travel three to four times farther than you do. Train your dog to come back when called. Only let your dog off the leash in a safe place away from traffic. Some city parks do not allow dogs to be off the leash.

Puppies

Your puppy cannot be taken for a walk until it has had all its shots. Until then, you can carry it around in your arms to introduce it to noises and smells in the outside world.

Older Dogs

As dogs age, they still need regular exercise. They might not walk as far as they used to, but they will enjoy going out. Walking will help prevent them putting on weight and keep their joints mobile.

Training

Training is an important part of owning a dog. A well-trained dog is a pleasure to know. A badly behaved one can be a nuisance. Reward your dog when it gets things right. If training is fun, your dog is more likely to learn.

Keep It Positive

Use a happy voice to tell your dog what you want it to do. Use the same words each time. Reward the behavior you want as soon as it happens. First reward small steps, such as moving in the right direction. Then reward the whole action, such as coming when called.

Rewards

You can use treats, toys, praise, or play as rewards for good behavior.

Housebreaking a Puppy

Learn the signs that your puppy wants to use the bathroom, such as walking in circles. Let the puppy outside and praise it when it uses the bathroom in the right place. Put down a sheet of newspaper if you live in an apartment. When the puppy has learned to use it, put the paper outside. Praise the puppy when it relieves itself outside.

Basic Commands

There are some basic commands all dogs should learn. These are coming when called, sit, lie down, walking on a loose leash, leave, and stay. When your dog has learned the basics, you can train it to do fun tricks such as shaking a paw.

Short and Often

Keep your training sessions short. Practice for a few minutes each time, several times a day. Before long, you will have the best-trained pooch in the neighborhood!

Keeping Healthy

Exercise, a balanced diet, and regular shots should keep your dog healthy. Even so, just like people, dogs get sick sometimes.

Fleas and Worms

Make sure your pet is up to date with anti-flea and worming treatments. Fleas can cause severe itching and allergies in your dog. Fleas can also pass on tapeworms. These parasites can cause illness if left untreated.

Skin Problems

When you groom your dog, look out for rough or red patches of skin. Also check for bald or thinning patches on your dog's coat. If your dog starts to scratch itself more than usual, or chews its paws, take it to the vet. In most cases, the vet can treat your dog's skin and coat problems with medicine.

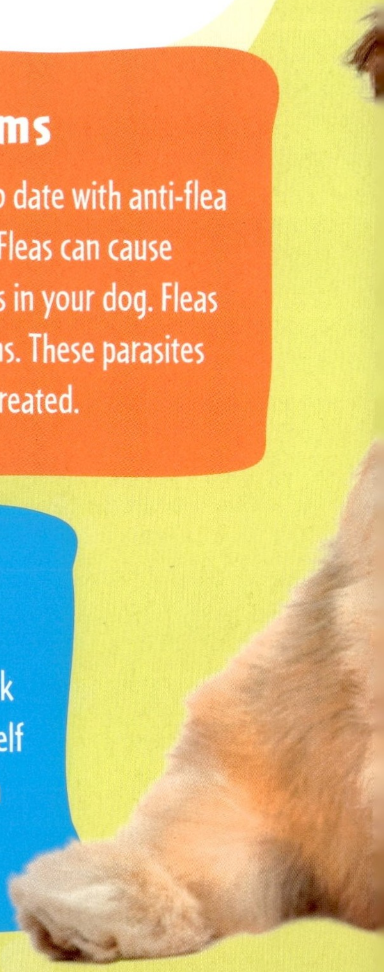

Shots

Puppies are usually vaccinated against disease when they are six to eight weeks old. They will need follow-up shots, and then booster shots every year to prevent disease.

Paw Problems

Check your dog's paws regularly for any problems. Look for cuts, scratches, thorns, or grass seeds. If your dog is constantly licking its paws, it may have an injury.

A Visit to the Vet

Take your dog to the vet once a year for its booster shots and a checkup. The vet will ask questions about your dog's general health and any problems it may have. Take along some treats so your dog has good memories of its visit to the vet.

Wild Dogs

People have been breeding dogs for over 10,000 years. Dogs were bred for different jobs, including hunting and guarding. All the breeds that exist today are descended from wolves.

Wolf Pack

Wolves live in packs of at least two animals, usually more. Each wolf knows its place, or rank. The strong, or dominant, wolves are called alpha dogs. They get first choice on everything, including eating first and choosing where to sleep. Lower-ranking dogs treat them with respect.

Dingoes

Dingoes are semi-wild dogs that live in Australia. They live alone or in packs of up to 10 dogs. As with wolves, there are alpha dogs and pack rules.

Your Pet Wolf

Most dog breeds do not look like wolves. But dogs' behavior and the way they communicate with each other are based on how wolves live. Think of your pet as a friendly wolf, and you'll get along with each other just fine.

The Pack Rules

- Don't feed your dog tidbits from the table.
- Don't let it sit on furniture or sleep on your bed unless it is invited.
- Feed your dog at feeding time, not when it demands to be fed.
- Teach your dog to wait while you go first through doorways.
- Use clear instructions and reward your dog when it obeys them.

The Family Pack

For your dog, your family is the pack. Your pet will pick up signals about who is in charge. It should be the lowest member of the pack. If a dog thinks it ranks high, there can be problems such as growling, snarling, or biting.

Labrador Retriever

The Labrador retriever, or Lab, is friendly, affectionate, and intelligent, and makes an ideal family pet. Labs also make excellent "seeing eye" guide dogs for blind and partially sighted people.

The Lab loves children.

Where in the World?

This loyal and reliable pooch comes from Newfoundland in Canada. Local fishermen used Labs to pull in their nets loaded with fish. Labs love water and go swimming any time they get the chance. They have a water-resistant coat, which keeps them warm.

Pet Care

Labs are patient, reliable, and gentle. They are best suited to living in a family house with a yard.

- Labs enjoy family life, are gentle with children, and are easily trained.
- Labs need plenty of space and exercise. They are not suited to living in a small apartment.

Profile

Labradors are strongly built. They are about 22 inches (56 cm) tall at the shoulder. The coat is short, straight, and thick. It comes in solid colors of black, yellow, or chocolate. Labs usually live 10 to 12 years.

Miniature Schnauzer

The miniature schnauzer is intelligent and playful. It is the smallest of three schnauzer breeds and makes a good pet. Farmers used these dogs to catch rats. They are also good guard dogs.

The miniature schnauzer is friendly and smart.

Where in the World?

The Miniature Schnauzer comes from Germany and was first bred in the mid- to late 1800s. It is a mix between the bigger standard schnauzer and smaller breeds such as the Affenpinscher.

Pet Care

The miniature schnauzer is a good family dog that enjoys company and family life.

- They make ideal companions for people who live in a city apartment, but they need plenty of activity to keep them from getting bored.
- The miniature schnauzer is a natural guard dog. It needs to be trained not to bark at visitors!

Profile

Miniature schnauzers stand about 12 to 14 inches (30 to 36 cm) at the shoulder. Their coat is short and wiry, and can be solid black, black and silver, or salt-and-pepper. They have very long whiskers and eyebrows. They commonly live to age 12 to 14 years.

Shetland Sheepdog

The Shetland sheepdog is playful and loyal. It was originally bred from larger rough collies for herding sheep. Also called the Sheltie, it is a popular family pet all over the world.

The Sheltie responds well to obedience training.

Where in the World?

The Shetland sheepdog comes from the Shetland Islands, off the northern coast of Scotland. The thick coat of the Sheltie is well suited to the cold winter climate of these islands. The islands are also home to a miniature breed of pony.

Pet Care

Shelties are loyal and good-natured dogs, and are gentle with children.

* They are often shy with strangers at first.
* Shelties are full of energy and need lots of exercise.

Profile

The Sheltie stands about 14 inches (36 cm) at the shoulder. It has thick white hair around the neck. The coat comes in different colors, including tan and white and black and white. Shelties live to age 11 to 13 years.

Jack Russell Terrier

The Jack Russell terrier is friendly and intelligent with energy to spare. These dogs suit an energetic family that has enough time for exercise, training, and play.

Where in the World?

The Jack Russell was first bred in England in the 1800s by the Reverend (Parson) Jack Russell. He liked fox hunting. The dog was trained to go down foxholes to chase out foxes. The dog had to run fast enough to keep up with the hunting horses.

The Jack Russell terrier loves to learn new tricks.

Pet Care

Despite their size, Jack Russells need at least an hour's walk each day plus training.

- They need to be occupied and should not be left alone for long periods. If they get bored, they will start chewing anything they can find.
- They can be noisy guard dogs, so they will need to be trained to stop barking at your visitors!

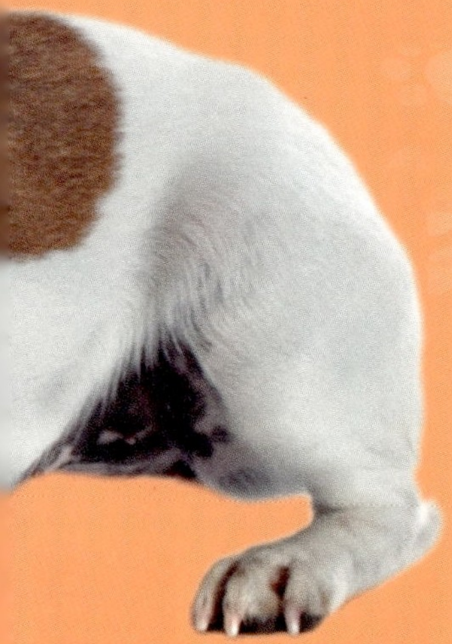

Profile

Jack Russells stand 10 to 14 inches (25 to 36 cm) at the shoulder. They have thick, smooth, or wirehaired coats. The thick coat keeps the dog warm in cold weather. Jack Russells are usually white with black, lemon, or tan markings. They live to age 12 to 15 years.

Easy-to-Make

Tasty Cookies

You can make these delicious cookie treats for your dog. Ask an adult to help when it's time to take the cookies out of the oven. Your pooch will love them!

You Will Need:

* 3 cups (360 g) whole wheat flour
* 1 teaspoon garlic salt
* ½ cup (120 ml) soft bacon fat
* 1 cup (120 g) shredded cheese
* 1 egg, beaten slightly
* 1 cup (240 ml) milk

1 Ask an adult to help preheat the oven to 400°F (200°C).

2 Put the flour and garlic salt in a large mixing bowl.

3 Stir in the bacon fat. Then add the cheese and egg.

4 Gradually add enough milk to form a dough.

5 Knead the dough and roll it out to about 1 inch (25 mm) thick.

6 Use a cookie cutter to cut out the dough or cut out shapes with a butter knife.

7 Place the dough pieces on a greased cookie sheet. Bake in a preheated oven for about 12 minutes, until they start to brown.

When they are cool, offer a cookie to your dog as a yummy treat!

Fun Facts

The American Kennel Club (AKC) currently recognizes 202 dog breeds. The Fédération Cynologique Internationale (FCI) is the biggest dog organization in the world. It recognizes 332 breeds. That is the number of breeds that most kennel clubs worldwide recognize.

Some popular new breeds include Labradoodles, Yorkipoos, cockapoos, and schnoodles.

Dogs have 42 teeth. That's 10 more than an adult human and 22 more than a child.

Dogs can hear sounds that are about four times farther away than humans can hear.

A dog's sense of smell is 10,000 to 100,000 times better than a human's. Some dogs have been trained to sniff out diseases such as cancer and diabetes in people.

About 44 percent of all households in the United States have a dog. That adds up to about 78 million dogs in the U.S. alone!

The average dog can learn 165 words. In the U.S., a border collie named Chaser was trained to learn more than 1,000 words!

Dogs only have sweat glands in their paws. They have to pant to cool down on hot days. It can help to wet the pads of your dog's paws when it's hot.

Glossary

breed (1) to take care of a group of animals to produce more animals of a particular kind. (2) a particular kind of animal that has been produced by breeding.

breeder person who breeds certain animals, such as dogs.

flea very small biting insect that lives on animals.

housebreak to train an animal to use the bathroom outside or in the correct place.

ID tag abbreviation of "identification" tag.

molt to lose hair and replace it with new growth.

parasite an animal that lives in or on another animal and gets food from it.

pooper-scooper device for picking up dog poop.

rank position in a group.

shots see vaccination

slicker brush brush with fine wire pins for untangling hair.

sweat gland area of the body that produces sweat.

tapeworm long, flat worm that lives in the stomachs of animals and people.

tick very small insect that attaches itself to a larger animal and feeds on it.

toxic poisonous or harmful.

undercoat a layer of short hair growing underneath the longer outer coat.

vaccination treatment with a substance, called a vaccine, to protect against a particular disease.

Further Resources

Books

Greenwood, Nancy. *My Pet Dog*. Buffalo, NY: Gareth Stevens Publishing, 2023.

Rossiter, Brienna. *My Pet Dog*. Mendota Heights, MN: Little Blue Readers, 2023.

Storm, Marysa. *Labrador Retrievers*. Mankato, MN: Black Rabbit Books, 2021.

Websites

10 Awesome Dog Facts!
www.natgeokids.com/uk/discover/animals/general-animals/dog-facts/
Learn more about dogs with National Geographic Kids.

Best Dog Breeds for Kids
www.akc.org/dog-breeds/best-dogs-for-kids/
Check out this list from the American Kennel Club with your parents or caregivers if you're trying to choose a dog breed.

Grey Wolf
www.dkfindout.com/us/animals-and-nature/dogs/gray-wolf/
Discover the grey wolf, a wild kind of dog!

Publisher's note to parents and teachers: Our editors have reviewed the websites listed here to make sure they're suitable for students. However, websites may change frequently. Please note that students should always be supervised when they access the internet.

Index